HOSPITALS

written
BY ROBYN GREEN

illustrated
BY LISA ARMITAGE

BOOKSHELF

Published by

Multimedia International (U.K.) Ltd

by arrangement with

Horwitz Grahame Pty Ltd

Distributed in the U.S.A. and Canada by:

Scholastic Inc.
730 Broadway
New York, N.Y. 10003
U.S.A.

Scholastic TAB Publications, Ltd
123 Newkirk Road
Richmond Hill L4C 3G5
Ontario, Canada

© Copyright 1986 text: Robyn Green
© Copyright 1986 illustrations: Lisa Armitage

Development and Management by:
Robert Andersen & Associates and Snowball Educational

Produced by:
White Kite Productions

National Library of Australia Card No.
and ISBN 0 7253 0813 3
Series (Stage 2) ISBN 0 7253 0806 0

Typeset by Bookset, Melbourne
Printed and bound in Hong Kong
by Dai Nippon (HK) Ltd
1 2 3 4 5 6 7 8 9 10 11 12
87 88 89 90 91

Acknowledgements:
The author, illustrator and publishers would like
to thank the Williamstown Hospital, Victoria; the
Prince of Wales Children's Hospital, New South
Wales; and Eunice Nash of Manly District
Hospital, New South Wales, for their assistance
in the preparation of this book.

Drawing on pages 18-21 by David Haylock.

Hospitals are very busy places.

Some patients are brought to hospital in an ambulance.

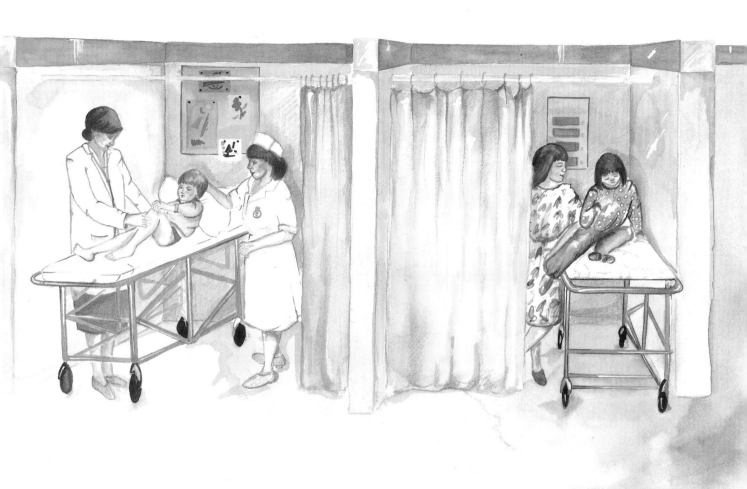

Doctors and nurses sometimes need to give emergency help.

Doctors examine each patient to find out what is wrong.

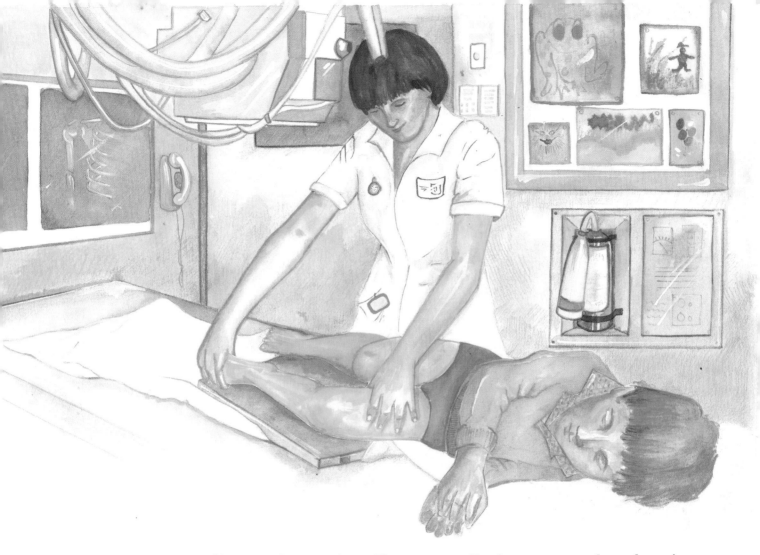

Sometimes the radiographer takes X-rays to find out exactly what is wrong.

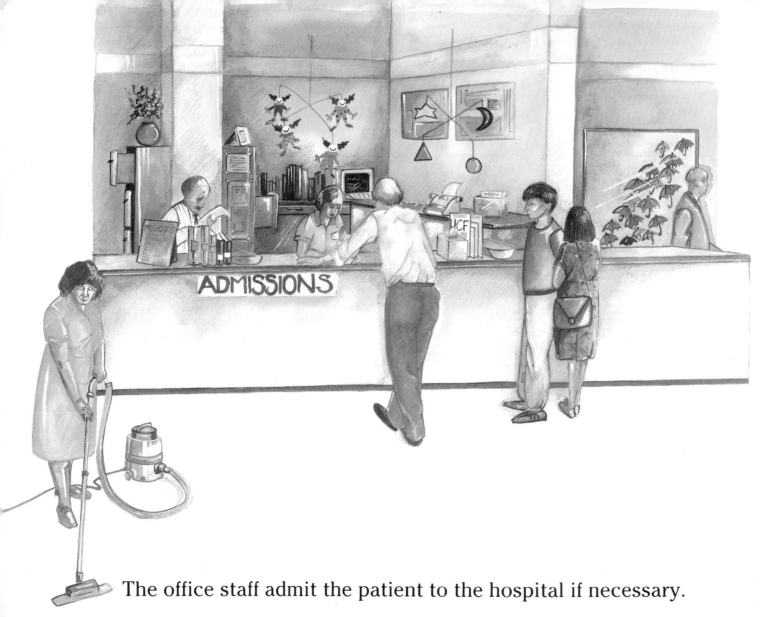

The office staff admit the patient to the hospital if necessary.

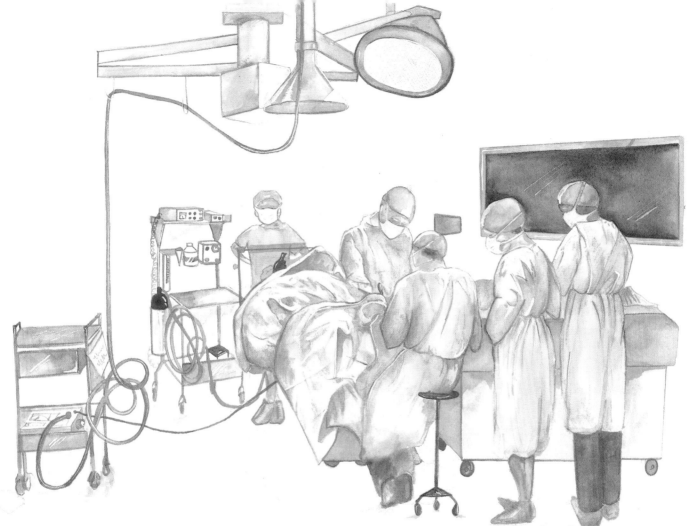

If an operation is required, nurses get everything ready in the operating theatre while the patient is being prepared. Surgeons then perform the operation.

In the wards, nurses give medication to patients and take their breathing rate, pulse and temperature.

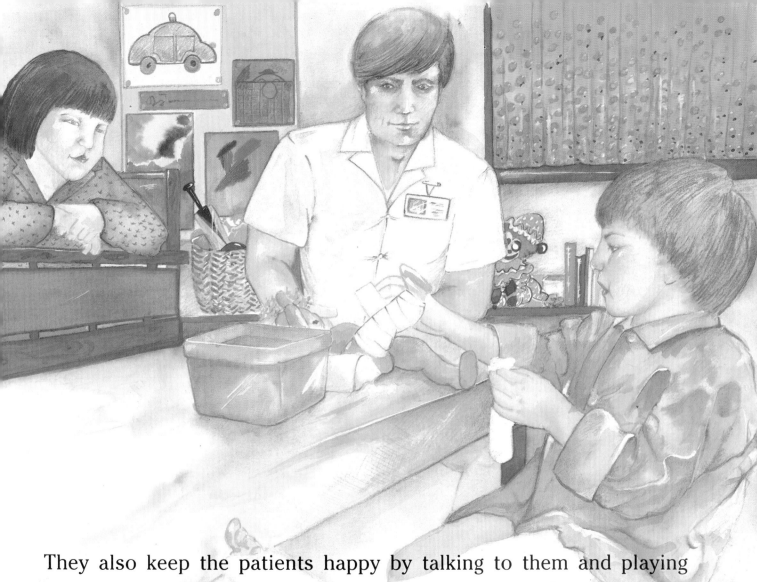

They also keep the patients happy by talking to them and playing games.

There are nurses on duty all night in case anybody needs them.

Some patients need to do exercises to make them strong again.

Cooks prepare the patients' food in the kitchen.

The catering staff deliver the meals to the patients.

The patients are allowed to have visitors every day.

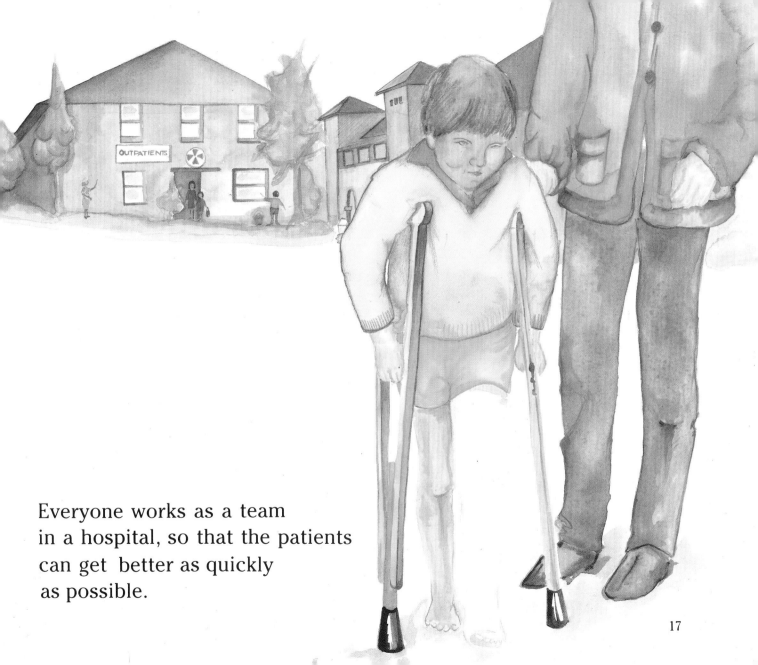

Everyone works as a team
in a hospital, so that the patients
can get better as quickly
as possible.

17

A Hospital at Work

LAUNDRY

KITCHEN

DELIVERIES &
STORES ENTRANCE